How Small Companies Get Big: A Simple Technique That Could Double Your Business

Category: Business & Economics

Author: Bob Oros

Publisher: Bob Oros Publishing

ISBN: 978-1-387-20128-0

Copyright 2017

Description: A large company has a CEO who creates a plan and presents it to the board of directors. They know exactly where they are going and how to get there. They have daily, weekly, monthly and quarterly reports to tell them if they are heading towards their destination. Learn a simple method to duplicate this strategy and watch your business grow.

Key words: motivating sales people, sales coaching, sales techniques, job in sales, sales manager training, manufacturing sales training, wholesale sales training, distributor sales training, food service sales, sales course, overcome objections, food sales jobs,

ISBN 978-1-387-20128-0

90000

9 781387 201280

1. How do small companies get big?

As I write this I am in Columbus Ohio and just took my rental car back. I didn't have to worry about how to find my way around because I had a GPS (Global Positioning System) telling me where to go. All I had to do was put in my destination and, like magic, I was given step by step detailed instructions on where to go.

Here's what I was thinking. "Wouldn't it be great if I had a GPS that would guide me towards my goal? I could program in my goal and get minute to minute feedback telling me if I am on course, or if I need to change direction or change my activities."

You and I actually do have a GPS already installed. It just has to be programmed. And once you enter your destination you will be guided with surgical precision.

The first part of the programming process is to choose a specific destination. It has to be specific. You can't program a GPS to head south; you have to enter an address, or at least a city. It can't be a destination that is unreachable or unclear.

In programming our personal GPS the input must be realistic, measurable, obtainable and most important, specific. You have either reached your destination, or you have not. There should be no gray area.

For example, you might program in more customers. However, programming in 250 more customers per week is a much more specific destination for your GPS to focus on. Same thing with programming in open a second location, or increase the size of every order. They are not specific enough.

Here's the main difference between small companies and large companies:

A large company has a CEO whose responsibility is to create a specific detailed plan and present it to the board of directors and stockholders. They know exactly where they are going and how they are going to get there. They have daily, weekly, monthly and quarterly reports to tell them if they are heading towards their destination. A small private company usually reports only to itself.

For a small company to really grow the first step is to prepare a presentation. One that would be detailed enough to sell potential stockholders on why they should invest their money with your company. Where you will be in six months, one year and five years from now.

Without a clear roadmap it is like a recent trip I took to Quebec. Everything was in French. I couldn't read a single road sign. If I didn't have my GPS I would have been completely lost. However, all I had to do was enter the address of the hotel I was heading to and presto, step-by-step instructions were given to me.

What is the address you want to end up at? Write it down. Give your mind a clear picture of what it looks like and presto! Step-by-step instructions will come to you almost like magic.

Comments:

I have created a profile sheet on every customer that I have ever seen. Every meeting and every phone call goes on that profile sheet for each customer, date I saw them and what we talked about. I write down everything, New that the customer is interesting in seeing anything the customer has concerns about. I write down everything, there birthday, holidays, day off. This is the information I keep on the customer. So on my next visit I am prepared for the customer.

Jim Harris

It never ceases to amaze me how effective it is to know something personal about the prospective customer and work it into the conversation. Recently, I called on the General Manager of a local defense contractor. He was very polite and listened to me for a few minutes but I could tell I was not getting very far with him. I mentioned to him that I had seen his picture on the Chamber of Commerce website as one of the Directors. I listened to him for the next fifteen minutes about his activities. It was very interesting and his tone was much more accommodating to me afterwards. We are all looking for ways to stand out in our customer's minds – to get them to lower that shield and dispense with the knee-jerk "thanks but no thanks" response. Doing just a little research can really payoff.

Crocker Smith

I was watching a special on espn about the retirement of Brett Favre. He has been in the NFL for 17 years and was explaining the preparation he goes through mentally and physically for each game. He cannot just go "wing it" in each game and expect to win. Of course sales does not have the physical aspect of football but does parallel the mental side. You have to have the mind set and information you need to win the account. You can never quit planning.

Gregg Nixon

Planning is important for any salesperson, whether they are a neophyte or seasoned sales professional. This is why email, computers, PDA's, laptops, CRM software, etc are so popular. They help us keep track of what we are doing, who we have business relationships with, and where we are going. I would wager that the longer you are in sales the MORE important planning becomes because theoretically the number of relationships and accounts you have should be increasing, meaning you would have more to keep track of the further you are into your career.

Marquesa Ortega

I may not actually keep a notebook of information, but I do have a manila file for each of my customers or prospective clients. I write information on these folders, and even if it looks sloppy, it does help me to stay organized. When I call a client, I have that file out, and all the info I need is readily accessible. You can really tell when somebody is paying attention to the small things; for example, when I go to visit my diabetes doc, she always asks me about stuff going on OTHER than my diabetes, and even though I only see her every 6 months, I really feel like she cares about me. I like her a lot. If I can get my clients to feel that way about me, I will do OK.

Laura J. Czajka

This is a great reminder lesson. I haven't been in sales very long or I am not "seasoned", but I already have seen myself cutting corners. Most of the time it will come back and nip you in the butt.

Dominick Yarnal

Planning is still the number one part of sales. You must always know what the prospects needs are in order to give a good presentation. Making notes on every conversation with each customer helps plan for the next meeting. Even the smallest details that a customer says can help you plan for the next sales call. You can pick up on concerns, objectives and be prepared to answer any question the client may have. This will help you understand what each customer wants or may need in the future.

Laura Arnett

Planning will always remain crucial. As sales professionals, we at times will feel we have much more depth of knowledge in terms of our products/services offered than the client. Most times this is true - and we often have the reps from the companies whose products we sell make presentations to us to brief us on the 'new lines'. This does not mean we do not need to plan our sales calls - any one of our clients could be very well informed and we could be left without answers, without the ability to give the service we may have represented.

I have learned alot from my clients about their specific uses/experiences with products. It is all a learning experience, but we should still take the time to prepare and plan - otherwise, why bother making the call, our time and the clients' time are both too important.

Wendy Parrott

2. When should you use a carefully planned pause?

When you use the pause, you freeze the sale for a moment. You step away, physically or psychologically, to review the work you have done up to that point and check over your plan for the rest of the presentation. You take a break. It may be purely mental, it may be imperceptible to the customer, but you give yourself whatever time it takes to review matters before you continue.

Using a pause gives you the opportunity to review the entire process of the sales presentation and to make sure that you are not overlooking anything. It allows you to avoid getting boxed into a corner. By using a pause, you keep your emotions from ruling the presentation.

Everyone has a different way of using a pause. Sometimes, how you pause depends on the situation.

In a selling situation, having someone with whom you have to consult before giving a final answer is a convenient excuse for pressing the pause button. Simply say, "I will have to run this by my partner (or consultant, sales manager, etc.) and get back to you at 9:00 tomorrow morning."

Taking notes is helpful at many points in a sales situation. One of the best times to pull out your pen is when you need to pause. Writing down statements that are confusing or upsetting is an excellent way to use the pause. Rather than stating an inappropriate remark, tell the customer to hold on while you write down the statement. Ask the customer to check what you have written to be sure that you got it right. The process of putting those words on paper almost always causes the customer to backtrack, amend, or, better yet, erase the words altogether.

Use a pause at each critical moment to review the presentation or to decide when to close a sale. Use a pause whenever you are feeling pressured or under stress.

Sales people can get caught up in the emotions of making the sale. They are afraid to lose. They fall in love with the idea of the sale and ignore facts that are important to decision making. They let their own moods, or the moods of the prospect, rule the presentation, causing things to wander off course. These problems disappear when you use a pause.

Pause before you give into a price discount. Your moment of reflection gives the price discount some significance. You must treat the discount as significant, or you are not perceived as having given a discount. No price discount is unimportant. By emphasizing each discount in your own mind, you have not given ground for nothing.

The obvious and easiest example is conceding a price too quickly. Too often, a quick response robs the customer of the good feelings that they get after making a good buy. It leaves the customer feeling that they could have gotten more if they had been smarter. Although that may be true, what advantage is it to you that they feel that way? None. Worse, now they are out to prevent that mistake from occurring the next time you negotiate, or they compensate by taking a hard line on another aspect of the sale.

Some buyers use pressure to get what they want from a sales person. Sometimes, the pause tactic is your only defense against being pressured into making a decision based on the buyer's deadline.

Comments:

Theatrics is a big part of the sales call, if you do not have props or samples, your actions and voice become your props. I sell in an area that is not familiar with my company, and it is important to listen to the customer, by pausing at strategic times, it gives the perception I am listening, and gives a chance for the customer to tell me what they need, sometimes without asking.

Gary Caudill

When you ask for the sale make them answer. Put out the question and then don't say a word. How you do it is ultimately up to you and how you think it will best fit the situation. If you break the silence you lose. I busted one of my customers yesterday for having a cooler full of my competitors product. I told him he was busted and asked him why. Then I let him answer. At the end of the meeting he said he would think of my company first for the products I carry. The silence forced him to realize he was "cheating" me of the sale.

Dave Ferren

A pause is a important tool in the selling process. In some cases when a customer is using it, a salesperson needs to understand this may be the customers way to take a moment to work through the information you have just give him or her.   Sometime you will find that during this 'pause' it is not the time to jump in and keep talking, or offering more things.   A pause for a salesperson is to reflect the information the customer has given us, and as this lesson states, it helps the salesperson to control the sales call.

David Vize

The pause works for both the buyer and the seller. Many times I have given a quote and the customer does not respond. This creates a tremendous desire to ask what they are thinking. Is the price too high? Is there something I could add to the deal to make it work for you? Ideally, you would like the customer to just say "okay, this looks good. Where do I sign?" And then you ride home thinking about where to spend your commission. It rarely works out this way. Let the buyer respond first and you have gone a long way to gaining the upper hand with the deal.

Crocker Smith

I had an incident in my previous job where I knew the client for a few years, and I knew they needed our product for their station upgrades. I made my presentation, and he said he needed me to come down on my price. I said that I had already given him a discount and I could not go down any further, along with all the benefits he would receive from the upgrade. Then the silence came. As uncomfortable as it was for me to sit there silently, I needed him to come to me with his response. We sat there in silence for 8 minutes! While I would never suggest doing that with a new client, I was comfortable enough with this client and his situation to know that he needed our solution and could pay our price. As I sat there in silence I was formulating other objection responses in my – but at the end of the 8 minutes (and I did discretely time this) he spoke first to break the silence and moved forward with the sale at my price.

Danielle Antonacci

After a customer comes back at you with a price that is below your target, its good to pause and let them think about the what they are asking of you. A long pause can kind of make them feel guilty for asking AND will usually prevent them from trying to whittle the price down further. It shows that the decision requires thought, and if you pause it doesn't make you look like you are so easy that you will reduce the price without question. A pause also allows you to formulate a response without speaking too hastily.

Marquesa Ortega

I really like the idea of taking a long pause before giving a price reduction. Of course, you should take some time to consider it, but when you extend it, it gives the impression that it is a really SERIOUS drop in price that you are thinking about agreeing to. Like the article said, it gives the customer a sense of satisfaction to know that they got you to agree to a drastic price drop, even if it isn't really all that drastic to begin with.

Laura J. Czajka

This is very interesting process. I never thought of using a pause when under pressure or feeling cornered. When I working in retail sales in the past the customer would try to get you to come fuller down on a product that was already discounted. Me being the manager at the time, I did not have someone to tell the customer I needed to consult with. I had to tell them no and take a chance of loosing the sale or make the decision to give them a bigger discount my self.

With Ambassador if someone calls me wanting to do business with us or wants a quote I have to get all there information and pass it on to our office sale manager. So using a pause to be able to write down everything I can get form the prospect for my manger helps a lot. The more information you can write down with help you or the sale manager be more prepared for the presentation.

Laura Arnett

3. Is there such a thing as a born sales person?

I am sure you would not like to have open heart surgery by a "born doctor" who understands the concept of open heart surgery but has never had any training? How would you like to get on an airline flight with a "born pilot" who understood the theory of flight but never had any professional training? How would you feel about eating in a restaurant run by a "born cook" who never had any training in food safety or proper cooking procedures. What about investing with a broker who "had a feeling" for the market, but had no professional training. Most importantly, when you are buying something, how do you feel about buying from sales people who do not know anything about their product except the price?

Careful planning will result in the skills and qualities necessary for success in selling. If you took a person who has never sold before and spent an entire Saturday planning every detail of what they were going to do during the next week, you would be amazed at the results.

Everyone who has been in sales for any length of time knows how to plan, however, we need to sell ourselves on taking the time and making the commitment. Once we sharpen our planning skills our work in sales will become more profitable and more enjoyable. To be considered a "Cutting-Edge" sales professional it is not necessary to work twice as hard as the "average" sales person, we only have to work twice as smart.

After three years in sales you will begin to feel confident. After five years it is very unlikely that you will ever want to do anything else for a living. If you take a walk through any bookstore and look and the success section, many of the titles hint on the idea that your sales success is guaranteed instantly if you follow their formula. Turn on the TV and during a commercial break all of your problems can be solved within 15 seconds after taking a certain pill. The generation coming into sales has unrealistic expectations of success, and when it does not happen instantly, they quit. Ask yourself: "How long do I think it will take to become a true professional in this business?" See how close you come to three years.

Careful planning will develop patience. As a "Cutting Edge" sales person, committing to a daily schedule is of prime importance; our success or failure in this area will have a major impact on our overall performance. We always plan tomorrow the evening before. Prioritize our goals. Make a list of all the things we want to accomplish and then rank them in the order of their importance.

On Friday evening or Saturday morning, prepare not only your Monday schedule, but also your schedule for the week to come. Do not feel you have to account for every minute of every one of the next five days, just block out your scheduled appointments and meetings so you have a good solid overview of what is on the horizon. Then review and prepare for each call you are going to make.

By attending to daily scheduling matters conscientiously, and comparing your actual results with your plan, you will increase your time-effectiveness and at the end of the day you will feel great, taking very little stress home with you. You will easily outsell the so-called "born sales person."

Comments:

I love to sell against the "Natural Born Sales Person" because they take for granted that people will buy from them. They are usually unprepared. Have little or no plan and spend lots of time boosting their own egos. Those guys are fun to steal business from because they always point fingers. I am very good with people but it is only the hard work and the attention to planning that keeps me going.

Dave Ferren

There are many stories of young athletes growing up who were great as kids. They had a natural, God given talent to hit or throw a ball or move around a basketball court with almost no effort at all and with great size. But for some reason they didn't want to play beyond the 8th grade. Why? Because they didn't want to do the hard work to get to the next level.

I'm sure we all have examples of great talent being wasted whether it be as a musician or an artist(graffiti guys come to mind). My point is that even if you are born with a talent, you must direct your energy to getting better each day because passion or God's giftedness will go to waste. There are many examples of people, who though they didn't have the greatest talent, kept working at it until they became successful; Michael Jordan comes to mind.

Are we all suppose to be sales reps? No more than I am suppose to be an IT guy. But if you have a passion for people (instead of gadgets), and want to help make their lives more successful by what you have to offer, then sales may be your vehicle to help them. But whatever it is, do it the best you can. Find the best there is and do what they do. My guess is that if you take Bob's advice, not only will you be successful, but satisfied.

Jim Ruth

Personally, I myself went from introvert to extrovert during my mid to late 30's. At various times prior to that I had been approached for different sales positions and I never saw myself as a salesperson. There are times now that I STILL don't. I more or less forced myself into my first job after discharging from The Corps. I was an extremely persistent salesperson for myself. Looking back upon the subsequent position changes I made (climbing the ladder) it dawned on me one day that I "sold" myself for each and every one of them, including the position I am in with the company I work for today. Not just passively selling myself, throwing in an application, showing up for an interview, nothing that simple. I had to overcome objections over lack of experience, black marks in my personal life, lack of formal education and even (in a few cases) the prospective employer not really having an opening or needing to hire.

I guess I'm validating the lesson in that I wasn't BORN to sell...I was MADE to sell.

Everyone on the planet has to sell in some aspect of their life. The lucky ones discover themselves in the process and go on to do so for a career.

Chris Chase

I think most people equate "born salesman" with confidence, charisma and gregariousness but also someone who is fast talking, loud and a back slapper. It is difficult to change your personality but through training, research and experience you can become a very successful salesperson. You may fly under the radar in comparison but your success will be built on a much firmer foundation.

Crocker Smith

The reason some people say that sales people are born is because they all share the same personality characteristics, such as the ability to accept no and keep on, and having thick skin. Some people may like the idea of selling and will try hard, but after being rejected several times, they get discouraged and feel they can't do it. Others have the tenacity to keep going. If we prepare, practice and push forward, eventually we will feel as if we are born to sell.

Kimberly Burgess

I agree! There are no born sales people. However selling is not for everyone. Its like any sport, anyone can learn it but you have to have the desire for that sport to excel in it.

Heath Blanchard

I believe people are more outgoing because of the environment they grew up in. Born Sales Person? A true sales person is somebody who is able to make the client or whomever believe that he or she believes in the product or service.

Personally, I never thought that I would be in a sales position but a lot of other people saw the determination in me that they thought would work in sales. I believe what may put me ahead of other sales people is that "no" just doesn't bother me. I know that what I have to offer is an excellent service, and as one the other managers said the other day. "I come with this service. You get a wonderful candidate, and you also get me." That makes sense.

Every sales person has something that makes them different and interesting to the clients or people around them. The way to succeed to find that something about you and build on it!!

Danah Parmley

I think everyone has very special gifts and talent and I do feel that some are just born to sell, love to sell and do a great job. I don't agree every person can be good in sales. Every person can not read music and every person can not play golf well. We all have talents and gifts. One can spend years mastering golf and still be very bad and just never get it. The same with anything, playing the drums MOST people don't have a clue and never will no matter how many years of training. So I do think you can be born a natural seller. I have friends who can read music and play any instrument and sing with no lessons at all, that is a gift that not all of us share. HOWEVER! I do think everyone sells all the time they just don't know what they are doing. (in their day to day lives) selling the kids to eat good food selling the husband to cut the grass ect. Selling mom or dad for that new MP3 player etc.

Ronda Kennesaw

I am a behaviorist by defined in the psychology world. I believe that behavior is learned. If a person is an extravert or introvert, it is because of their life's experiences (Environment). Environment is key to the success of any individual. If you hung out with the "wrong crowd" in high school or college, there is a great chance that you did not graduate. Sales people develop over time within their environment. Some environments allow people to excel more than others. Take for instance the sales environment for Ambassador. We have some of the most professional and seasoned sales people in the industry. The seasoned sales professionals (Owner, Corp VP's, Regional VP's) at Ambassador all posses the same common trait. They all have put in many hours and years of perfecting their craft. Some bring certain things to the table and some bring other qualities to the table. Most importantly, I feel that all the seasoned sales professionals have a high level of empathy. They were once on that bottom rung of the corp ladder and the majority of them have not forgotten where they came from. They too were just days, months, and a year into sales.

Jeffrey Mole

I must agree that there are no " born " sales people. The work ethic or your make up of who you are and your attitudes towards life in general are a product of your environment, however you can change if there is enough commitment and motivation from within.

I always considered myself an excellent " meat cutter " " butcher " .Yet I was not raised in a slaughterhouse or on a farm, however I spent many a summer on my grandparents farm. I enjoyed cutting meat and the discipline of butchering. To me it became and still is a true art form if you apply yourself and practice……practice and learn and grow. I still learn new things about the art of butchering and enjoy learning about it even though I have not picked up a knife in almost 6 years, why ? It became an intricate part of me .This skill would not have be developed without sweat , commitment and sacrifice ie (openness to learn and work)

I play guitar by ear, people I know say I am good but without practice and commitment I can never develop the ingrained talents that I apparently have. I play for the shear enjoyment, and with my life today I simply can not afford the time and commitment to consistently practice and hone my skills so the chances of me ever going on tour with Eric Clapton are very slim. However I have developed a skill level . I play considerably better that I did 10 years ago, when I got the guitar, how did that happen , practice and just doing it ....and enjoying the ride.

We all have various talents, skills , but with out first recognizing the talent , and constantly practicing and honing the skill and truly enjoying the process, the talent will never reach the potential that it was destined to.

Alex McQueen

4. What do your customer want from you, a sales person?

What are the things customers want from a sales person? The only way to know for certain is to ask them. I did just that and here is what they told me.

1. "Do not sell me - help me buy. Give me a choice between something I want and something else I want and help me decide what is best. Do not try to push something on me just because you want to sell it."

One of the things buyers really dislike is a pushy sales person. There is no faster way to damage the relationship than to apply too much pressure on your customer. Our job is to sell, however, business to business selling is much different than the "one call close" type of selling. During a one call close presentation the sales person knows that once he or she walk out the door of the prospects home the sale has ended. Many of the sales training programs we encounter are designed on this type of selling, as are many of the books we read about selling. There is a big difference.

2. "Do not sound like you just graduated from selling 101. Do not use timeworn techniques to pressure me to buy when I do not want to. Sound like someone trying to help me. Sound like a friend."

Again, we must set aside many of the basic selling tactics used in consumer selling. For example; the use of a "tie down" question. Here is how it works. A customer asks you if the product comes in a number 10 can. You respond with: "would you like it in a number 10 can?" This response makes you sound like an amateur. How should you respond? "Yes Bill, this does come in a number 10 can. It also comes in a plastic pouch. Would either one of those work out for you?" Only a slight difference, however, the first response implies pressure without having all the facts, while the second response implies that you are interested in helping them make the best choice.

3. "Be sincerely interested in what I do. My business may not seem overly impressive to you, but it is everything to me. Be interested enough in my problems to ask questions and help me find solutions."

The old school of selling used to teach us to have a high self interest. I remember one training school I attended where the instructor told me to visualize "My money is in the customers wallet - my job is to get it!" That works well when selling used cars or furniture, however, that type of attitude will destroy a relationship as well as a career in sales that require long term relationships. It is up to you to know the difference.

4. "Do not talk down to me or tell me what I am doing is wrong. I want to feel good about the choices I have made. If I have made a mistake, be tactful. Show me how others have made the same mistake."

This desire on the part of the customer is simply to deal with a sales person who is considerate and tactful. No one likes to make a mistake; however, if you have never made any mistakes you have never done anything worthwhile. When pointing out a mistake that a customer is making, do it with extreme tact.

5. "Reinforce my decision to buy from you. I need to be reassured that buying products and services is my best alternative. Do not take my business for granted - let me know I am appreciated."

We are all guilty of taking our best customers for granted. Once a customer has been buying from us we have a tendency to let up and take it easy. We forget that our competitors are calling on them and giving them the attention they crave. If we take our customer for granted we are very likely going to be left out in the cold.

6. "Do not tell me - show me how you will service me after I commit to writing checks totaling thousands of dollars every month. Do not forget me after the initial sale by putting me on automatic pilot."

There is an old saying that is very applicable to today's business: "What you do speaks so loudly I cannot hear what you say." Empty promises and good intentions simply do not keep the business. Even if we have a good relationship with the customer it can dissolve in a heartbeat if we do not take care of their needs and help them achieve their goals.

"Tell me success stories. Tell me about similar situations where someone using your products and services is having success. I do not want to be the first or the only. I will have a lot more confidence if I know of others who purchased and are doing well."

Once we make a sale the job is only beginning. We have to keep our customers sold and this requires reselling them every week. Talk about the successes people are having with your products and your company. When you or someone in your company opens a new account, do not keep it a secret. Customers like to deal with someone who is successful.

7. "Give me proof. I want to believe what you say, however, I have heard it all. I need facts and information that back up the statements you make. Show me a letter from a satisfied customer. I want reassurance and justification the price I am paying is fair for what I am buying."

Always back up your statements and claims with proof. When presenting new products do the required homework. Get the facts and figures to back up everything you say. Do not just rely on your relationship with the customer to make the sale. Show them you care enough to do the homework.

Comments:

A check list is good to have. It is like when you buy a house, you have to go through a check list to close the deal. You want to make sure you cover everything off the list. This no different when you getting a new customer or selling something to a customer. People don't want to be pushed in to something that they don't want. The customer has to believe in you and have that comfort level to buy from you.

Jim Harris

Just about all potential customers you call on do not think that you will do the seven things that they want in a sales partner. If they were convinced you would do these things for them you would not have to make any sales calls because they would all be calling you. Obviously, our biggest challenge is to somehow convince and influence the customer that we can and will do these seven functions and we will do them better than anyone else. Bob's survey is extremely valuable. We should all probably tape it to our dashboards.

Crocker Smith

"Treat others as you would want to be treated." Many times this quote never makes it to the business world. In sales the buyer needs someone they can TRUST. When you are able to have a buyer commit to your service this is only the beginning. The feeling you get when you close a deal is the same feeling that buyer should have after you have delivered your service. The same praise you get from your boss after closing a deal is the same praise that buyer should get from his boss for picking your service. I feel what buyers really want is to have no regret.

Heath Blanchard

Recognition, acknowledgment, reinforcement, patience, honesty and sincerity. Really, what we all want from people we are dealing with. We've all gone out to purchase something in our personal lives and we've all experienced a salesperson that left a bad taste in our mouth or actually prevented us from buying from them – so we know what not to do. It's a relationship, not just a sale. The biggest thing we can do is truly hear what the client is saying – not just listen but really hear... by doing this we will have a true understanding of their position and needs and we will be able to move on appropriately from there.

Buyers want us to treat them as we would want to be treated – not as another sale.

Danielle Antonacci

"A comment about the total package, or building process that is needed to make a successful sale.

Like building a house, every segment of the building process from foundation to framing to wiring to shingles on the room must be followed in order to have a strong efficient structure. Any short cuts usually result in an inferior building and a less than successful sale......Sure you may get the sale , but what did you give up?

Alex McQueen

5. Do you believe in superstitions?

For the past several years I believed that I could not sell any of my sales training programs and keynote talks during July and August.

"They" said everyone is on vacation. "They" said no one has sales meetings in the hot July and August months.

I decided to challenge my thinking and see if there really is such a thing as the "summer slump."

I made extra calls and put in a little extra effort. Low and behold - I made a sale. Then another and another. It turned out that July and August were my best months of the year!

I couldn't stop there. I looked in my history books to see what was done during the hot "Dog days of summer."

Here is what I found...

The heat of southern Spain did not force Columbus to wait until "Labor Day." He sailed July 22nd!

George Washington did not retire to the shade of Mount Vernon when it got hot. He took active command of the Continental Army on July 3rd!

During the dog days of JULY and AUGUST the Puritans set sail for the new world!

Our forefathers met and signed the Declaration of Independence!

Singer sold his first sewing machine...

The first section of the Atlantic cable was laid...

Lincoln began his debates with Douglas in the July heat of the Illinois prairies...

The first oil was struck at Titusville...

Meade defeated the Confederate Army at Gettysburg in July...

The first street car line was operated in this country...

Europe began the greatest war in history...

The French Revolution was started in July...

The first locomotive steam train chugged out of a Baltimore station for the West - in July...

July and August were the "golden days" for the forerunners of the modern sales representative - with everything in the back end of their buggies from lightning rods to chewing tobacco.

Forty-two thousand gold seekers crossed Death Valley to California in 1850 when the temperature hung around 130 degrees... in July and August!

August, 1902, the Cadillac Automobile Company was formed.

August,1914, The Panama Canal is inaugurated with the passage of the steamship U.S.S. Ancon.

"Wait until after Labor Day!" "They" say.

"There is not any business now!"

"No use killing oneself in this weather - nobody buys until fall!"

The next time the friendly competitive sales person edges over to you in the lobby and admits there is nothing doing until after Labor Day, encourage him or her in this delusion.

AND THEN SLIP OUT AND MAKE THE BIGGEST SALES OF THE YEAR - BEFORE LABOR DAY!

The bottom line - DO NOT BELIEVE IN SUPERSTITIONS! SELL 52 WEEKS A YEAR!

Comments:

You can sell any day of the week and any week of the month and any month of the year. As long as there are customers, there are sales to be had. All's remember that. I here that all the time, no sales in July and August I even here no sales in December because of Christmas. As long as you knocking on the doors and customers are letting you in, you can sell anytime. I know people go away on

41

holidays but the world doesn't stop. You have to go out and shake the brushes to see what comes out. Make the extra calls and you will be surprised in July and August the customers you find still working.

Jim Harris

A few years ago a customer came to my house at 8:30pm New Year's Eve and signed an order for an $85,000 tractor. I was taking a few days off and was not expecting any more business before January. This helped him with his taxes and pushed me over the top to win a sales contest for that year. He could have come Christmas morning at 7am and it would have been fine with me.

Crocker Smith

"Sales" is whatever you make of it. So is life!!!

"Usually during the months of November December months things tend to get a little slow with the staffing industry." I have heard come out of my mouth many times as well as other co-workers that I have worked with.

Then somebody proves you wrong. I hired a Branch Manager in October. He closed two Direct Hires in December. How did this happen? Motivation and Ambition!!

He didn't care how slow people thought it was going to be, he was just out there selling.

I am such a believer in that fact that if you think something is going to happen it will. If you think you are getting sick, then you probably will be.

If you think you are going to close business before the end of December, then you will. Making it happen!!

Danah Parmley

"I can say one thing about this lesson. The 'dog days of summer" is the best time for my sales. From the end of February to the middle or end of November is the best selling time for me. Then in December and January I work extra hard and sell payroll accounts. Then it's back to fulfilling all the "temp to hire" needs and securing new accounts. I can't say that I have hit a low period for sales yet. I'm not saying that every week is booming, however, it is always important to work new angles. I may sign my biggest account in December. That will be such a thrill for me and our office. Sometimes your best sell is the one you have had to work the hardest and the longest on. This is when you know that it was all worth it. "

Patsy Clements

"When the summer months hit, in the foodservice industry our reps are usually extremely busy with seasonal accounts, increased business , along with increased business comes the increased daily challenges etc. that occupy a distributor sales reps time making it difficult to pursue the new business………. but it is vital to note that our competitor reps are also facing those exact situations so it makes sense that the opportunity to get new business is there if you are in the right place at the right time. "

"The only way that you will be in the right place at the right time is to place yourself there. The customer is too busy to call you so they put up with the situation and they may call you in the fall when there business is slower …or they may have forgotten the situation in the summer and decided to leave status qou."

"I everyone is busy especially your competition with day to day tasks ………………..there is the opportunity for the individual who is committed to his or her craft."

"You get out of …………………….What you put into."

Alex McQueen

I have witnessed the "dog days of summer" first hand. Maybe everyone gets excited with the warmer temperatures, people taking vacations; it is more of an "outside" time of year. No matter what time of year it is business still must operate, and thrive! Though we tend to think that our efforts are useless at the time, every effort and contact we make for business always pays off down the road. It is never too soon to start making your contacts!

Brooke Knight

I've been told over & over that the end of the year is not a good time to sell our services because everyone is planning for their holidays, closing out their books for the end of the year, planning their budgets for next year etc... I believed that until last year when I was able to acquire my biggest service fee. Buyers do not base their buying habits on the time of the year; they base it on the time of their need.

Carla McCrea

About the author Bob Oros

Regardless of whether you are reading one of his books or attending one of his programs, the most frequent comment is: "This guy has been there, he is one of us, I am going to use these strategies."

With over 2,000 speaking engagements in all 50 states and several international locations for manufacturers, distributors and associations, you can be sure you will get the results and information you are looking for. Prior to starting his speaking career, Bob served six years in the US Navy as a Communications Specialist and then worked his way from a street sales person to the position of National Sales Manager for a Fortune 200 company.

Bob has received awards for speaking, writing and marketing too numerous to mention.

Additional Topics by Bob Oros

Why Sales People Fail

The Key to Selling Anybody

The Power of Expectations

Add Value to Every Product

How to Justify Your Price

Lost in 60 Seconds

One Good Reason to Buy

Control a Buyer's Attitude

How to Create Demand

Smoke Screen Objections

Take the Risk Out of Sales

How Small Companies Get Big

How to Create Demand

Overcome Every Objection

Take the Risk Out of Sales

Small Companies Get Big